Moving Beyond Treeline

Meanings of a Wilderness Experience

Larry Beck

For Andy

For Dan and Leo

And for my students

-LB

*   *   *

Let us probe the silent places, let us seek what luck betide us;
Let us journey to a lonely land I know.
There's a whisper on the night-wind, there's a star agleam to
guide us,
And the Wild is calling, calling...let us go.

-Robert Service

*   *   *

Contents

One
Voyageurs

Page 1

Two
Paddling

Page 9

Three
Olesen's Place

Page 25

Four
Portaging

Page 33

Five
Aki

Page 45

Six
A Complete Desolation, A Northern Fairyland

Page 49

Seven
Rescue Free Wilderness

Page 55

Eight
The Country, The Space, The Sky

Page 65

Nine
Wolf Pups

Page 71

Ten
Afterword

Page 77

Notes

Page 83

Great Slave Lake

Chapter One

Voyageurs

*Though he is one of the most colorful figures in the history of a
great continent, the voyageur remains unknown
to all but a few.*
-Grace Lee Nute, *The Voyageur*

No roads lead to Dave Olesen's place. He lives in a cabin
along the shore of Great Slave Lake, deep in the wilderness of
Canada's Northwest Territories. Great Slave Lake, named for
the native Slave Indians, is among the ten largest freshwater
lakes in the world. It is 300 miles long and up to 140 miles
wide, with a depth of more than 2,000 feet. The lake is so
remote that it was not completely surveyed until the early
1920s. The surrounding landscape is mostly flat, spangled with
other lakes, large and small. Stunted black spruce forest gives
way to treeless tundra further north. Here is one of North
America's last great refuges for wildlife: tireless wolves and

lumbering grizzlies, ungainly moose and sparring caribou, bald eagles and wailing loons.

I am a member of a group of canoeists consisting of 12 men and two women. From the community of Yellowknife, to the west, we have paddled 210 miles to Olesen's cabin. Although fully versed in the mechanics of backcountry travel in canoes, we are anything but an athletic and youthful crew. Ranging in age from mid-thirties to early sixties, we have worked hard to get here.

We are delivering three handcrafted cedar-strip canoes. Olesen is hoping to establish a supplemental income during the summer months as a wilderness outfitter and canoe guide in the "barrenlands" of Canada. Just north of his cabin, about 70 miles, is the northern limit of trees and our final destination with the canoes.

As suggested by their price ($2,500 apiece) these are not ordinary canoes. They were built by members of the Minnesota Canoe Association over the course of a year. Many in our group were involved in crafting the canoes and have a due interest in paddling the finished products. Each canoe is 24 1/2 feet from bow to stern, specifically designed for long expeditions on vast lakes.

On the water, laden with four or five paddlers and three weeks of supplies, the canoes are stable and seaworthy. Moreover, the artisanship of each craft is striking. The cedar strips mesh together like the narrow slats of a fine, polished hardwood floor.

This trip was planned by co-leaders Leo McAvoy and Al Gustaveson. Leo is a university professor and Al is a carpenter, under whose direction the canoes were built. The remaining crew consisted of avid canoeists with a diverse range of vocations, most all from Minnesota, the land of 10,000 lakes.

Leo called me several weeks in advance of the trip knowing I'd be interested. With the encouragement of my wife, six months pregnant, I accepted Leo's invitation. I took a flight to our starting point in Yelllowknife, via Edmonton, from San Diego. The rest of the group drove from Minneapolis in a crowded van. They hauled the gear and canoes in a trailer. With a rotation of drivers they were northbound for 56 hours, traveling non-stop except for gasoline and meals, churning up road dust over unpaved highways.

*　　*　　*

Sigurd Olson, one of America's eloquent interpreters of wilderness, wrote in *The Lonely Land:*

There are few places left on the North American continent where men can still see the country as it was before Europeans came and know some of the challenges and freedoms of those who saw it first, but in the Canadian Northwest it can still be done.[1]

Indeed, this adventure is reminiscent of the journeys of early explorers and voyageurs (a French word meaning "travelers") who paddled northern lakes in the heyday of the fur trade from the mid-1500s to the early 1800s.

The fur trade came about as a consequence of the search for the Northwest Passage, a channel between the Pacific and Atlantic Oceans. Jacques Cartier explored the St. Lawrence River, what he believed to be the Passage, in 1535. Although he didn't find the elusive passage, he traded with the natives who were eager to barter for iron kettles, knives, hatchets, wool cloth and other manufactured goods.

The natives traditionally cooked by dropping hot stones from a fire into clay vessels or tightly woven baskets. Imagine the convenience of using a metal pot over an open flame. Or using a steel-bladed knife to skin an animal, or an axe to fell a tree, rather than crude stone implements. In exchange for these luxuries the natives offered, among other things, beaver pelts that were hailed back in Europe as an ideal felt for making hats. The fur enterprise continued to expand to the north and west as hunting and trapping depleted nearby beaver—and fox, lynx, wolverine, river otter, and wolf.

Transportation along the "voyageur's highway"—an intricate system of lakes and rivers—was straightforward. Just as American pioneers moved west in covered wagons, the voyageurs paddled north in canoes over established routes.

The canoes were made from forest materials. Birch bark, fitted over a frame of cedar boards, was sewn together with the root of a conifer (often red spruce) and caulked with the melted gum from pine trees. Canoes varied in size from the enormous "Montreal" canoe (35-40 feet) that hauled five tons to the "North" canoe (25 feet) that could carry one-and-a-half tons.

The vessels were well cared for. Voyageurs were careful not to run their boats into shore or paddle in high winds. An oilcloth was carried for covering the freight and, on occasion, for raising a sail. Large sponges were used for bailing.

Voyageurs considered themselves fortunate to engage in physical, outdoor work. The hardships of the business were dismissed; rarely did voyageurs complain. They boasted about their feats of strength and often tried to outperform each other. Those who showed fatigue during the day were ridiculed.

Because of the tenor of their work voyageurs fulfilled two criteria for hire. They had to be short, on average five and a half feet, so their legs could fit comfortably in a canoe without taking up precious cargo space. Furthermore, they needed strong arms and shoulders in order to propel the canoe *and* carry goods overland between lakes or around rapids. Periodic obstacles to clear and open paddling required hauling (portaging) the canoes and gear.

Freight was packaged in 90-pound sacks. One sack was lifted onto the back, then another was hefted on top for a standard load of 180 pounds. A tumpline (a strap across the forehead and attached to the load) was used to ease the burden. Incredibly, some men could carry three sacks and, rarely, as many as four. Twisted ankles and bruised feet were common and injuries from falls under enormous loads killed some voyageurs. Only drowning in dangerous rapids claimed more lives.

During the long light of the summer months, voyageurs spent upwards of 15 hours per day transporting their goods over land and water. A sense of urgency tended to pervade the enterprise. On the water voyageurs took some 40 strokes per minute, in unison except the steersman, to average five miles per hour. At portages the canoes were quickly unloaded. Then the men took off at a trot under heavy loads. Over long portages the canoes and gear were carried perhaps a half-mile at a time. Once the full load was gathered it was moved another half-mile. It took several trips back and forth to move the entire load. Upon reaching navigable water, canoes were reloaded and launched again.

Voyageurs took breaks on the water periodically to rest tired arms and shoulders. Pipes were lit and stories told for about 10-15 minutes. Voyageurs rested as long as it took for a pipe; once the smoke cleared it was time to move on.

At camp, a typical meal was a thick soup of peas, strips of pork, and biscuits all mixed together in a large pot which hung over the fire. Etiquette varied. In some instances the canoemen all sat around the kettle taking spoonfuls at a rapid fire pace.

Sometimes dishes were used. In other cases the whole meal was poured out on flat rocks (in order to cool faster) and the voyageurs lapped it up like dogs. Afterwards, pipes were lit.

Voyageurs took great joy in taunting each other. They were, in a word, playful. Around the campfire they told exaggerated stories in which, inevitably, the storyteller was the hero. They doled out nicknames to each other in direct contrast to some physical trait.

To pass time on the water voyageurs burst out singing. Songs ranged from hymns to patriotic ballads. The general favorite was "A La Claire Fontaine" ("At the Clear Running Fountain"), a love song that in no way was related to the voyageurs' day-to-day life. Voyageurs also sang about those things around which their work revolved. All in all it was a good life as suggested by the following testimony:

> Said one of these men, long past seventy years of age: 'I could carry, paddle, walk and sing with any man I ever saw . . . No portage was ever too long for me. Fifty songs could I sing. I have saved the lives of ten voyageurs. . . Were I young again, I should spend my life the same way over. There is no life so happy as a voyageur's life.'[2]

The paradox of this happy life is that it revolved around hardship and danger. Voyageurs experienced the rewards of an outdoor lifestyle—a joyous state that comes from exercise, fresh air, comradeship, simplicity, and freedom. They were blessed with timeless days on the water, in full song, amidst a backdrop of exhilarating beauty. Yet this was complemented by depravation and exposure to those same natural elements which could kill them. These seemingly contradictory forces contributed to an exuberant lifestyle that wasn't, perhaps, otherwise possible. Their highs were appreciated more since they also withstood the lows and understood the risks associated with what they were doing. They lived on the edge and would have it no other way.

On the Water

Chapter Two

Paddling

*The voyageurs suffered as all men do when they move into
lands they have never seen before, and they epitomize in their
own way what has motivated all adventurers since the
beginning of time. The land they explored had a certain genius
of its own but was marked forever by their passing. Those
who are fortunate enough to pursue any of these trails become
part of the ancient dream.*

-Sigurd Olson

Like the voyageurs we are delivering goods—in this
instance the canoes. Like the voyageurs our labors are
physically demanding. Like our counterparts from the past we
have a routine. And like the voyageurs we are travelling
through a landscape where nature's rhythms dominate. Unlike
the voyageurs, we have volunteered our efforts. Most of us had
figured this might be fun.

Wake-up call is at 5:00 in the morning. By no later than
6:30 or 7:00 we have loaded and launched the canoes, having

broken camp and eaten a breakfast of cereal, usually, and coffee. We take short rests on the water every hour or so, the canoes huddled together for variable periods of time.

We usually cover 12 to 14 miles before stopping for lunch. As we are weary by midday, lunch is followed by a short nap. We sprawl out almost anywhere and sleep for a half hour. Our progress is less remarkable in the afternoon as we continue to wear down. By evening we make camp: pitch tents, gather wood, build a fire, fetch water, prepare dinner, clean up, fall asleep.

On camping ventures I prefer to sleep out, under a sky of stars, rather than within the confines of a tent. Here we bed down in tents out of necessity. The climate in the Northwest Territories is variable. We will endure many nights—and days— of rain. This is also the time of year when mosquitoes and blackflies flourish. (The mosquito netting on the tents is designed to keep insects out.) Finally, there are no stars to look at, even given a cloudless sky, because it does not get dark this far north in July. One member of the group became the subject of well-deserved ridicule when he admitted he brought a flashlight.

*   *   *

It is our first evening on Great Slave Lake and I wish I had known to bring my own tent. We have seven tents and sleep in twosomes. Like most of the tents here mine is sturdy and will sleep three or four; for two it is spacious. The tent I now share is, by a considerable margin, the smallest here. It sleeps two bulgingly. For lack of space one person enters and gets settled, then the other. During the course of the journey this tent will leak rain through the sides. Mosquitoes and blackflies will mysteriously enter through the fabric at night. The very last evening the center pole will snap and the tent will collapse entirely in the midst of gale winds and heavy rain.

At the moment my dismay is focused on the actions of my newly acquainted tentmate. His name is Dan. He is large, strong. Dan has discovered, this first day of our journey, that his boots leak. As I enter the tent, having sat a short distance away enjoying the rich light of late evening, I see that he has just finished patching his boots with rubber cement. Surrounded by boundless terrain he has chosen, to my astonishment, the inside of our shelter for his task. It is too late to suggest another plan; the tent is rank with glue fumes. This first night I have strange, glue-inspired dreams and wake up with a headache and sore throat.

*   *   *

The second day finds us still seeking the optimal arrangement of crew so that the boats are evenly manned. The canoes have four paddling stations; two in front and two in back. There is room for one paddler in the far front of the bow and, just behind, there is sufficient space for two paddlers, side by side. Likewise there is one paddler in the stern, the captain, and space for two paddlers just forward. In the mid-ship of each canoe is storage space for our gear.

We have concluded, so far, that one canoe will bear the four largest men, each in a paddling station, one behind the other. With some experimentation we have also determined that the other canoes will have three small paddlers up front and the remaining two in back, one behind the other.

I occupy the position in front of the stern in a canoe of five. Behind me is Tom, tall and lean, in a red wool shirt, cleaving the water with long, powerful strokes.

Tom tells me has been married almost 20 years. He and his wife have created a lifestyle that celebrates the past. Together they researched, obtained plans, and built an 18th century Cape Cod house on their 60-acre property in Independence, Minnesota.

From the maple trees on his land he makes his own syrup. His wife plants "antique" flowers in their garden; that is, flowers that were commonly grown when America was first settled by Europeans. Another of their pastimes is putting together "antique" meals. Elaborate menus were recorded back in the 1700s and through diligent efforts Tom and his wife have duplicated a George Washington Christmas dinner. Cooked in the traditional manner, this feast offers a half dozen main courses and just as many desserts.

The meals planned for this trip are hearty and substantial, although otherwise no relation to Tom's banquets. For dinner we have "one-pot" meals. Spaghetti. Linguini. Macaroni. Other nights we eat chili or stew with cornbread or biscuits. The baking is conducted "dutch oven style," using coals above and below a covered pan for uniform heat. Fresh-caught lake trout, northern pike, and arctic grayling supplement the planned menu. The critical factor, and this can't be overstated, is that there is plenty of food. We eat like voyageurs.

There is always a pot of coffee and something for dessert. Brownies or cheesecake. Gingerbread or mousse pudding. Our first night out we ate two Jack Daniel's pecan pies, baked and given to us by one of Olesen's friends in Yellowknife, to christen the journey.

Tom and I continue to talk as we ply open water. The members of this canoe have made several shifts of position from yesterday's arrangement and there is a considerable difference in our performance today. Everything has come together and our group is paddling as one. In full synchronization, we are cutting swiftly through the water. The momentum of the canoe is bracing as we move through the cool morning breeze.

Indeed, we are outpacing the others. Looking back we see that they have fallen far behind. We stop to let them catch up. They are lagging again shortly. Once more we stop. It is obvious, now, that our canoe team is stronger. The other paddlers are killing themselves trying to keep up. There must be an exchange of personnel, for balance.

I find myself in the same position in another canoe. Now Leo is behind me. Leo is a solid outdoorsman—compact, sturdy. He is soft-spoken with dark, graying hair and beard. He was an officer in the Navy.

Leo is a professor at the University of Minnesota. He pushes students under his charge, though in a benevolent manner, and not beyond their capabilities. It is a delicate balance and he will employ the very same ingenuity in motivating this group to reach its destination.

Leo takes this assignment seriously. Dave Olesen wants the canoes delivered north of his cabin to Maufelly Bay on Walmsley Lake. Leo said we could do it and he intends to see that it happens. Leo understands the variables that may delay us so he *constantly* pushes forward.

The co-leader of the trip, Al, is Leo's lighthearted foil. Al is buoyant and playful. His beard is full and gray, his crown balding. He is a diminutive man, gnome-like, full of songs, tales, and laughter. He speaks convincingly on most any subject. He is sinewy and strong. In proper garb, a few hundred years ago, he would offer the personality, stamina and size to have passed for a voyageur.

We paddle on, passing through clusters of small islands, eventually stopping on one to eat. Lunch is mostly an assemblage of high energy food: peanut butter and jam on biscuits, crackers and cheese, dried fruit and nuts, cookies and hard candy. As we eat we are scolded by arctic terns. They scream at us, swooping menacingly from above. They are protecting their nests that are on the ground and contain three or four mottled, dark green eggs. The eggs are well-camouflaged in the rocky tundra; so much so that one is accidentally stepped on.

We have been drawn here, most of us, out of wonder and respect for the landscape and its wildlife. That deference seems compromised as we paddle away from the island, leaving behind a crushed egg and the hysterical cries of the terns.

The sky is gray when we land for the night and we eat our dinner through a drizzle. I drift to sleep to the patter of rain on the tent.

*   *   *

We break camp and launch the canoes in an early morning shower. The rain is not hard enough to keep the mosquitoes down. My arms and shoulders are sore and my legs cramped, as are everyone's, as we break into the cadence of paddling.

Al notes, in reference to the tight quarters of the canoes and our physical labor, "What hurts is everything between my neck and my toes."

A cloud of mosquitoes follows each canoe as we leave the mainland. Paddling in the cold rain, enduring the infernal mosquitoes, I reflect there are only 19 days to go.

Mosquitoes are as much a parcel of the north as the wolves and caribou, the unnamed lakes, the steel cold winters, the northern lights. The natives of this land, the early adventurers, and all those who have followed suffer the presence of these winged pests.

In 1833 George Back launched the first exploration into the barrenlands, seeking the mouth of the Great Fish River. He wrote in his journal: "There is certainly no form of wretchedness, among those to which the chequered life of a voyageur is exposed, at once so great and humiliating as the torture inflicted by these puny blood-suckers." He added, "They convey[ed] to us the moral lesson of man's helplessness; since with all our boasted strength and skill, we were unable to repel these feeble atoms of the creation."[3]

In 1907 Ernest Thompson Seton set off on a voyage to study caribou and other aspects of the natural history of "the arctic prairies." He devoted an entire chapter of his subsequent book to mosquitoes. Seton liked to document hard numbers. He devised, of all things, a "mosquito gauge" in which he held up his bare hand for five seconds and then counted the number of mosquitoes on the back side. Although crude, his method did provide a relative measure of the abundance of mosquitoes. He found that the concentration at the start of his journey, in Saskatchewan, was mild, in the range of five to 10 mosquitoes, compared with that further north. On Great Slave Lake, in July, the numbers reached 50 to 60. Seton wrote, "It was possible to number them only by killing them and counting the corpses."[4] Still further north, in the barrenlands, the hand test revealed 100 to 125 mosquitoes.

Seton also calculated the number of mosquitoes on his tent. He registered 30 mosquitoes on six square inches of the fabric and, as the tent was uniformly covered, came up with

24,000 mosquitoes over the entire surface. At one point, Seton counted "a round 400 mosquitoes" boring away on the jacket of the comrade paddling in front of him.

To ward off mosquitoes and blackflies we carry plenty of insect repellant. We have loosely woven string jackets, soaked in repellant, that we wear over our clothes. We have fine-mesh headnets to cover our faces and necks. And still the infuriating pests hover and penetrate.

With no inclination to tally the number of mosquitoes on the backs of those in front of me, my imagination wanders as we slog on.

We reach Mile 60 of our journey by the end of the day. We unload the canoes in a light shower. The rocks are slippery and several people take hard falls. Then the skies begin to clear.

There will be a little free time before we prepare dinner so I piece together my fishing rod, attach a bright lure, and promptly land three arctic grayling. The fish are filleted, along with some lake trout that someone else caught.

We place the filets in a plastic bag, then in a large pot which is sunk just offshore with a rock on top. This way we do not needlessly attract wildlife, like bears, and the lake refrigerates the fish. The water is biting cold—indeed, there are still a few ice floes on the water in July, a reminder that the surface is frozen throughout the winter.

*   *   *

We have fish and potatoes for breakfast before breaking camp, then paddle the canoes through a thick, early morning mist. The air is moist and cool. Piercing the shroud of mist, the sun punches through fingers of light, which radiate from the sky like the spokes of a wheel.

An old friend once told me that this is called the "God effect." The divine rays brush the water.

The lake is calm as the fog vanishes. The water is as smooth, and as reflective, as a mirror. It is as if we are paddling in animation through clouds floating above *and* drifting below us.

The calm morning becomes increasingly breezy and we are windbound by afternoon. Most of the crew gathers together near the canoes. I hike up a hill to a vantage point, a nook in the rocks. I can see the flotilla of canoes far below. Starbursts of sunlight sparkle on the waves in Hearne Channel. A long, narrow island—Blanchette Island—forms the channel. There are delicate puffs of clouds in the pale blue sky. Closer, birch leaves flutter in the wind. The cool breeze is refreshing in the intense, powerful rays of the sun.

As the wind subsides, late in the afternoon, we paddle onward. Just before landing for the night we see two bald eagles high in the trees on McKinley Point. Their head and tail feathers catch the serene evening light. The eagles fly from one perch to another, but not away from us, as we drift silently in awe.

Our response to the wildlife is in contrast to that of the early explorers here. In George Back's journal he recounted sighting a "majestic fishing eagle" seated in a tree. His men flagrantly shouted at the eagle to frighten and flush it. I can imagine the scene, the men carrying on like stooges, the product of a different time, a different mentality. As Back reported, the eagle "unscared by our cries, reigned in solitary state, the monarch of the rocky wilderness."[5]

It is time to find a camp. The terrain is rugged and it takes some scouting to locate a suitable site.

On the fifth day we paddle 23 miles following our now well-established routine. After dinner we gather for a camp meeting. Leo seems pleased with our progress so far. In five days we have covered 103 miles. We are almost halfway to Olesen's cabin. It is good fortune that the wind has not held us back any more than it has. Leo reads us an excerpt from George Back's journal. Then Al breaks out a worn copy of *The Collected Poems of Robert Service*. He reads "The Lure of Little Voices," an excerpt of which follows, that sums up why so many of us are here:

Yes, they're wanting me, they're haunting me, the awful lonely
places;
They're whining and they're whimpering as if each had a soul;
They're calling from the wilderness, the vast and God-like
spaces,
The stark and sullen solitudes that sentinel the Pole. . .
It's the lure of little voices, it's the mandate of the Wild.[6]

I spent a summer in Alaska many years ago working at Denali National Park and Preserve. A few verses from Service's "The Spell of the Yukon" sum up that experience and why I was so eager to return to the sub-arctic.

The summer—no sweeter was ever;
The sunshiny woods all athrill;
The grayling aleap in the river,
The bighorn asleep on the hill.
The strong life that never knows harness;
The wilds where the caribou call;
The freshness, the freedom, the farness—
Oh God! how I'm stuck on it all . . .

There's a land where the mountains are nameless,
And the rivers all run God knows where;
There are lives that are erring and aimless,
And deaths that just hang by a hair;
There are hardships that nobody reckons;
There are valleys unpeopled and still;
There's a land—oh, it beckons and beckons,
And I want to go back and I will . . .[7]

Such is the magic—the lure—of the far north.

*   *   *

It is Sunday, a day of rest. We paddle 15 miles before stopping for lunch, then set camp on an island. With the afternoon for leisure I take a dip in the lake, lathering and rinsing afterward with a large pot of water on land. Then I launder my clothes, again on shore, and set them on rocks to dry. Refreshed, I assemble my pole and fish until I've caught two lake trout.

Popular wilderness sites show wear from an onslaught of recreational use. On this trip we follow "leave no trace" strategies to protect the pristine environment. Although we are far removed from civilization and relatively few others travel here, out of habit and respect we minimize our impact.

Bathing, laundering clothes, or washing dishes with soap can suds up a lake or stream. This not only affects the aquatic ecology, it provides evidence that others have traveled through. So, we wash away from the water source and use biodegradable soap. Likewise, we keep our fires small and collect only fallen, dead wood. This practice helps conserve dwindling wood supplies.

*   *   *

Well rested, we paddle 27 miles, to Mile 145, over the course of a clear day with cool breezes. We approach Plummer's Outpost which is a "resort" for people who are flown in for the good fishing. We see, occasionally, motorboats carrying fishing parties. This is a different approach to experiencing the landscape.

At Plummer's, patrons sleep and dine in the rustic complex and are, therefore, more removed from the rhythms of the sub-arctic summer. By day they zip around in motorboats from cove to cove using sonar devices to locate fish. Guides navigate the water for the paying customers. The landscape passes quickly as the boats dash about under the drone of outboard motors.

On a prominent rocky point we see huge boulders covered with lichens. Carved into the spongy lichens are names and dates. This form of vandalism is representative of a different creed. It is a self-absorbed ritual, a proclamation for all to witness, "I was here."

As we paddle past the dock of Plummer's Outpost, we can see the lodge in the background. Someone on shore hollers out to us, "Where are you going?"

Al calls back a lie, "Baker Lake," which is hundreds of miles to the east, almost to Hudson Bay.

Just past Plummer's we spot a black bear. From this point on there is almost no presence, or evidence, of other people.

*   *   *

This morning we paddle 10 miles to the Mountain River. George Back, in his early exploration, vividly described a prominent mountain here, yet with even the wildest use of our imaginations we never see it. The wind picks up and we are once again windbound for the afternoon.

Snow in deep packs covers the ground. We explore a cabin, now in total disarray, abandoned by a miner. Sorting through the debris I can imagine the rusticity and solitude of living here. Within this evidence of the past, history comes alive. In this cabin I can see and touch the lifestyle of a miner long ago. Historian David McCullough noted, "We need the past for our sense of who we are ...[and] because it is an extension of the experience of being alive."[8]

Dan, my tentmate, fishes a pool where a river enters the lake. He makes five casts and reels in five fish. Then we move on to our camp for the night.

$*$ $*$ $*$

The ninth day we paddle toward a solar halo, a ring of light around the sun with faint rainbow colors. According to northern lore this forecasts a violent shift in weather.

We stop for lunch on an island known as Bigstone Point. A red-throated loon flies over us low and menacingly. We are near her nest. We see a single, large egg at the edge of a pond. The pond sits in the middle of the island and we are on the opposite side of the nest. I feel an ineffable sense of tension as the loon comes at us again and again.

Suddenly, our oldest member, Venice, begins violently choking. He is above everyone else, high on some boulders. Leo bounds up to him, determines he is gagging on food, and applies the Heimlich maneuver. The first abdominal thrust is ineffective. Leo is more forceful in his second attempt as Venice struggles for air, but this too fails to dislodge the food in his throat. The third thrust is a mighty, desperate attempt to save Venice. It works and Venice can breathe again. Although he is clearly shaken up and in pain, he handles himself as if nothing has happened. I talk with him, uncomfortable with his nonchalance, as others glance nervously toward us. (Upon our return to civilization x-rays revealed that the abdominal thrust that saved Venice's life also broke one of his ribs.)

We camp for the evening next to a large cove where several of us swim, briefly, in the shallow, frigid water. Waves from one to two feet break on the unprotected shore like the crash of ocean surf.

One member of the group has been saving something special—a bottle of brandy, a vintage from long ago, a pricey gift of appreciation he received from a business transaction that saved a company a lot of money. We drink with gratitude as the amber light of the sun reflects off the cliffs on the other side of McCleod Bay.

*   *   *

On the next day, our tenth, we arrive at Olesen's place, 210 miles from our starting point.

Olesen's Cabin

Chapter Three

Olesen's Place

We choose our own reality, our own path, each one of us.
Or by default we follow a path set out before us. I have chosen
this life. It is a rich and good one.

-Dave Olesen, *Cold Nights, Fast Trails*

As we approach Olesen's cabin we set off the howling of some 30 or 40 dogs. Olesen is a dog musher. He breeds, trains, and races sled dogs. His work demands living on the northern skirts of civilization.[9]

Among other long-distance races Olesen has competed in the Iditarod Trail Sled Dog Race, the 1100 mile Alaskan race from Anchorage to Nome, and the 350 mile John Beargrease Sled Dog Marathon along the north shore of Lake Superior in Minnesota. Unlike a human marathon, which is completed in a couple hours, the major sled dog races take several days. The winning time for the Iditarod is about a week-and-a-half. Sled dog racing demands the endurance of the Tour de France and is similarly dominated by a few big names and a large field of lesser-knowns.

On shore we are greeted by three friendly puppies, and Olesen, who heard the commotion. The puppies, energetic and playful, scamper about our legs.

Olesen invites us to look around his property. He owns but an acre of land, which is a moot point, since he has no neighbors. Olesen has lived in his cabin for three years. For transportation he has a plane, a motorboat, a canoe, and the dogs. He fishes and hunts. He can kill one moose per year and unlimited caribou. The butchered meat he keeps outside in a cache, an elevated platform for storing food, that is inaccessible to wildlife. The outside temperature is so cold that the meat stays frozen through the winter. Any day a barge is due to deliver 10,000 pounds of dog food and 1,200 pounds of dry groceries to supplement fish and wild meat for the coming year.

Olesen is, by his own definition, thrifty. He has to be. To field a competitive sled dog team is expensive. Only the top dog mushers earn much from race purses and generous sponsorship is hard to come by. Since seasonal work is necessary for a predictable income, Olesen is buying these custom-built canoes to launch a venture called Et-Then Expeditions Ltd. He will offer "journeys of adventure and education in the far north." Et-Then means "caribou" in the Chipewyan language. Much of the cultural and natural history of this region revolves around the caribou. Et-Then canoe routes and base camps will be influenced by the movements of caribou herds.

Olesen is good at cutting corners. In the days to come I note he always wears the same work clothes. He recently let his airplane mechanic cut his hair and it looks like it. He has traveled with his dogs by truck, by boat, by plane, and by train. Most often he is on the road in beat up pickup trucks overflowing with dogs and gear. Traveling to and from races, Olesen and his partners are inclined to drive nonstop. Camping by the side of the road in the middle of winter isn't promising and motels are too expensive. So he and his friends just keep driving.

Although Olesen may be thrifty, he isn't cheap. With all the vagaries of his line of work Olesen notes, proudly, that at present he is breaking even.

Olesen has the fortune, or the bane depending on perspective, of a physical lifestyle. His subsistence ways and upkeep of the kennel translates into hard work. He chops firewood for winter temperatures that drop below minus 40 degrees Fahrenheit. He maintains his cabin and outbuildings. He hauls food and water every day for his dogs. He uses a shovel often.

Olesen is, as much as one can be nowadays, self-sufficient. Compared to what most of us are accustomed to his lifestyle is remarkable in its simplicity. If he needs something he cannot rush to the store.

Olesen accepts uncertainty. He answers to the rhythms of a desolate, uncompromising, yet stately, land. He has a sense of place. His lifestyle keeps him strong. He is removed from the congestion, the pollution, the clamor, the frenzied pace of society as most of us know it. In the autumn, when snow has fallen and the lakes freeze, Olesen thrills in swift and silent travel behind a team of dogs.

There is both art and science to Olesen's work. Many still hold images of dog-driving when large dogs, kept in line by whip and club, pulled heavy loads during the gold rush days storied in Jack London's *The Call of the Wild* and *White Fang*. Now, smaller, faster dogs are employed in racing teams, and cruelty and neglect have been replaced by affinity and care. At all major sled dog races veterinarians conduct, among other things, blood tests to check for prohibited drugs.

There is a strong bond between most mushers and their dogs. The most successful long distance racers consider everything from dog nutrition, to athletic training techniques, to obedience, to canine psychology. Olesen strives to breed dogs that are tough, fast, eager, and responsive. The puppies cavorting at our heels will make up teams of the future.

Olesen's log cabin is laid out like the letter "T." The stem serves as the living quarters with a wood-burning stove, a table, and provisions. The room which branches to the left is a study, full of books. To the right is a small bedroom.

On the other side of the cabin are plywood dog houses, spaced evenly in a sandy area. The dogs are chained and have run of a small radius around their shelters. Today the dogs are mostly sedate. By sub-arctic standards this sunny afternoon, maybe 72 degrees, is a sizzler.

At the far end of the dog yard is a wolf that paces incessantly. Olesen found a wolf den and took two young puppies, a male and female, from a litter of four. The male escaped. Olesen's desire is to breed the female with his dogs. He figures that 1/8 wolf could provide for certain desirable characteristics in a line of sled dogs. He also tells us that the native Inuits are opposed to the keeping of wolves. He rationalizes keeping this wolf because so many people in the far north kill them to cash in on $400 per pelt, and keeping a live wolf, by comparison, seems reasonable.

Unlike the other dogs, which are domesticated, the wolf is clearly unhappy and behaves neurotically, like a caged animal in a zoo. Watching this one pace, its nervous energy, its longing to be free, I can't help but feel pity for the creature and a certain appreciation for the native wisdom.

After setting camp in the woods most of us take a swim in a sandy cove. Later, several of us gather to hear Olesen share tales of his three years here—working the land, taking caribou and moose, encounters with bears, a mink that got into his cabin. Then we return to our camp for the night.

*   *   *

Today we will leave Great Slave Lake. We have just a three-mile paddle before we begin portaging—carrying the canoes overland from lake to lake to our final destination which is 70 miles to the north.

Leo follows the canoes in a small outboard boat that will serve as Olesen's transportation back to his cabin at the end of the day. I am paddling just in front of Olesen who has taken Leo's position in the stern and is handling one of the canoes for the first time. The water is rough; the most turbulent we have paddled in. The blustery weather would have kept us ashore if not for the short distance to our first portage. As we pass close to a point of land, the waves reverberate off the rocky cliff, the turbulence pushing the canoes like a rolling sea.

Before moving to the Northwest Territories, Olesen lived in Ely, the same town in northern Minnesota that writer Sigurd Olson lived in. Of only a few select books in his cabin's bedroom are three or four by Sigurd Olson, who was instrumental in the efforts to preserve Minnesota's Boundary Waters Canoe Area Wilderness.

Olesen left Ely, a relatively quaint town to an urban observer, because of increasing commercialism and what he perceived as "trendiness" and "cliques." Likewise, he is concerned that more people are being attracted yet further north for the wrong reasons. He tells me he worries about yachts on Great Slave Lake and people coming to play golf at midnight on Ellesmere Island. He doesn't believe this land should be utilized to fill a void for those who would come expecting to be entertained.

Olesen is drawn by the remoteness and a lifestyle that is conducive to raising and training sled dogs. He is not a hermit, he enjoys company, although he suggests this would be a good place to be a hermit. Olesen, however, is married. He met his wife, Kristen, at a wedding. To bring in much needed income Kristen is a cook at a mining camp, far away for the summer, although she is taking some time off to join us for the last few days of this journey.

Portaging the Canoes

Chapter Four

Portaging

So dat's de reason I drink tonight
To de man of de Grand Nor' Wes',
For hees heart was young, an' hees heart was light
So long as he's leevin' dere—
I'm proud of de sam' blood in my vein
I'm a son of de Nort' Win wance again—
So we'll fill her up till de bottle's drain
An' drink to de Voyageur.

-William Henry Drummond

Our first portage is two miles overland from Great Slave Lake to the first of a series of unnamed lakes leading us north. According to Olesen this particular route to Walmsley Lake has never been done before.

Each portage requires three trips to the next lake. The first trip is an overview of the route in which we carry our personal packs (clothes, a sleeping bag, camera, fishing gear and so on). The second leg we transport the canoes and assorted community gear including food packs. The last trip we carry a collection of leftover packs and whatever else remains such as canoe paddles, life vests, and the wanigan—a scythe-shaped wood crate which fits snugly in one canoe and contains an assemblage of awkward gear including a saw, a gas stove, pots, pans, and other cooking supplies.

To advance these two miles actually requires a to-and-fro total of 10 miles; five times the mileage gained. This first portage will consume an entire day. For long portages, such as this, we break the labor into *stages* that provide more frequent "rests" as we walk back to pick up another load. We haul all of the gear about a half-mile before moving on.

Carrying personal packs and food packs is relatively easy although one member, an avid backpacker, observes that this is the first time he has ever carried a load that he can't lift himself—a food pack weighing 100 pounds. More difficult is carrying the canoes that weigh in the range of 175 pounds.

Each canoe is hoisted up and over by four or five people and set on the shoulders of two carriers. A yoke, attached to the canoes for portaging, fits on the neck and shoulders of each carrier; one person in front, one in back. Only seven of us (and Olesen) are strong enough to share the weight of a canoe, for any distance, and are, therefore, almost always members of the three pairs who advance the beasts.

Leo and I are a team for this portage. We set out like oxen, heads inside the canoe that rests upside down on our shoulders. I am in the front and can see only a few yards ahead since the overturned canoe blocks most of my view. We follow someone carrying a pack who helps to direct us over the route.

The canoes, so graceful on water, are cumbersome and awkward on land. The weight bears down, focused on our shoulders, like a vise. Often, the burden shifts entirely to opposite shoulders of the carriers; my left shoulder, Leo's right.

Frustrated, we blame each other for a problem that turns out to be consistent among all partners.

It is not so much the weight or pain that bothers me as the fact that carrying the canoes through this terrain is dangerous. Every step must be deliberate, for to falter would be to get crushed beneath the bulk of 175 pounds of cedar. In the first stage of this portage the footing is difficult. We walk a route that parallels a ridge and the ground is as solid as a wet sponge. Our feet sink with every step. The second stage is even worse—through a swamp. I step high, as a moose would, over the hummocks and into the wet bog.

It is raining now, pattering on top of the canoe and draining down the sides. The water runs down my wrists where I hold the canoe and gathers in my rain jacket at the crook of each elbow. Upon setting the canoe on the ground at the end of this stage I pour a pint of water out of each sleeve.

The next stage offers solid footing along a sandy esker, a ridge deposited by streams under glacial ice long ago. On the first trip (with a pack) of each stage I develop a habit of noting a certain landmark along the route, toward the end, to gauge when we will be close to putting the canoes down on the second trip. For this advance my marker is a wild rose, the fragile petals knocked to the earth by the force of rain.

A colleague in Alaska, who became close to me as a friend, gave me a drawing she said was special to her. A line sketch of roses, the caption read: "Wild roses bring happy thoughts." As we carry the canoe past the wild rose in preparation to finally set it down —wet, weary, shoulders throbbing—these words ring true.

The next stage of the portage continues along the esker to our camp for the night. After setting camp on higher ground we move the canoes through another swamp to the lake in which we will launch them in the morning. We eat under a tarp, protected from the rain, then retire for the evening, completely spent. Olesen, meantime, has gone all the way home to feed his dogs.

*   *   *

We launch the canoes in the morning and commence a series of portages from lake to lake. Olesen joins us once again. From his cabin he took his motorboat to the portage, then hiked to our camp. He has a small canoe with him that he can carry alone and he will return home this evening, re-tracing our path over land and water.

On land we follow a network of caribou trails, so well-traveled that in places the path is 15 inches deep. There is evidence of caribou everywhere. Antlers, fur, and scat. We are in the midst of millions of pellets, like black jellybeans, scattered across the landscape.

The trees are mostly alder and black spruce. Closer to the ground is labrador tea and blueberry. Carrying the wanigan with Olesen over a short portage, he notes this will be a good year for blueberries, which he collects as they ripen at the end of the summer. Later, while portaging a canoe, he recites "The Voyageur" from a collection of poetry, *The Habitant*, by William Henry Drummond. Habitants were French settlers in Canada, many of whom became voyageurs. Leo, charmed by the verse, expresses an interest in seeing Drummond's work. (A few days later Olesen will fly over our camp in his plane to check our progress and to drop a plastic jug into the water, full of fresh brownies and a book of Drummond's poetry for Leo.)

We face a strong headwind and whitecaps on the last lake for the day. At camp the wind is so fierce that a gust dislodges and blows away a tent (which is subsequently retrieved) that was staked into the ground. It begins to rain as we prepare dinner. Gingerbread and coffee for dessert rekindle our spirits.

After dinner I walk along the lakeshore, alone, in a light sprinkle. I stop to watch an arctic tern fishing. It is patrolling the length of the lake. The flight is purposeful, the strokes of the wings deep. It is hunting for small fish and insects. Several times it dives, stopping short of the water. Then, while I am standing motionless, it hits the water in an explosion directly in front of me.

*   *   *

This new day we continue to leapfrog a series of lakes. Paddle and portage. Paddle and portage. It rains intermittently all day and the winds become progressively stronger. Whitecaps begin to form on the water as we face strong headwinds. I ask Leo, an accomplished sailor, about the velocity of the wind which he supposes is 30 to 40 miles per hour.

The day is cold and damp; the mood is somber. At one portage Al, carrying the stern end of a canoe, sinks knee deep in muck and has to be pulled out.

One person, who has distinguished himself as being outmatched by the conditions, feels compelled to verbalize his misery as we start yet another portage.

"Now my rain pants are slipping," he complains. "What else can possibly go wrong?"

The voyageurs of past centuries would have been ruthless. To the credit of several men on this trip our complainer has been handled with kid gloves, and in retrospect he will forget the hardships. At this point in the trip, however, he is miserable.

At dinner we flip a canoe on its side and extend a tarp from it for shelter. Several people snuggle into the gut of the canoe, others scatter under the tarp near the fire. After everyone else has gone to bed I stay up with Leo and Al and we talk, wishfully, of reaching the Hoarfrost River.

It is important to Leo, especially, that we get the canoes to their destination. We told Olesen that we would deliver them to Maufelly Bay on Walmsley Lake and Leo wants to honor that. (This is also where we have made arrangements for pick up by a Twin Otter plane that will land on the water and carry us back to our starting point in Yellowknife.)

*   *   *

After a windy night Dan opens the tent flap and reports the weather. It is cold. In the 40s. Cloudy. Looks like rain.

We break camp and paddle across a lake to face a long portage through thick vegetation. So we can follow the most direct route we tie bandanas on stunted spruce trees at strategic points to guide our way. On higher ground we build rock cairns, three rocks one atop the other, as markers. Navigating the route is still a challenge.

Having advanced our personal gear, Dan and I set out with a canoe. Our navigator loses the route and it slowly becomes evident that we are lost. Rather than wander about aimlessly with a canoe on our shoulders we set it down and determine our bearings. We are far off track. This is a tough portage and the extra effort we have caused ourselves is demoralizing.

As we enter the next lake we face our stiffest headwind yet. We paddle, making progress by the inch, until our arms feel like jelly. We come around a point and enter the next lake through a narrow channel just deep enough for the canoes. We had anticipated this being a short portage and are delighted to slip through without unloading and transporting all the gear. As we paddle to the end of the next lake it looks as if we might be able to slip through another narrow channel, but the water is too shallow for the fully loaded canoes. Rather than portage we hop into the frigid water, to lighten the load, and push the canoes through.

After paddling across another lake we stop for lunch. Several people sack out on top of the packs. Shortly, we walk over the portage to assess the wind, which is fierce and kicking up whitecaps on the water. Waves one to two feet high are crashing on the rocky shoreline. At the head of the stream between the two lakes is a protected, calmer site where it might be possible to load and launch the canoes, one at a time.

Al dreads fighting the wind again and questions whether we are capable of getting across the lake, even assuming we can launch the canoes. Leo thinks we can do it; we've had lunch, we've rested, we're on a mission. Al walks away silently with his dissenting opinion and comes back over the portage hauling a canoe.

We set the first craft on the water for loading. Leo is in the water, immersed near to his waist, holding the canoe against the shore—otherwise it would be smashed against the rocks in the channel. All loaded, the first canoe sets out with slow, but steady progress. We repeat the procedure with the second canoe. The last canoe is ours. Leo keeps the canoe steady, near the bow, as we load and get in. As Leo releases the boat we paddle furiously to avoid being blown into the rocks and as the canoe passes Leo he dives into the stern. It was a tricky maneuver and we break into a chorus of cheers as we edge out into the lake.

We next face a series of short portages. Over the shortest, Al and I team up to carry two canoes, one after the other, just to say we did it.

After the last lake we make a half-mile portage over stable terrain to our camp. The wind is blowing hard. It is difficult carrying the canoes because they are picked up off our shoulders by the wind like unwieldy kites. Two canoes make it over to our camp, the last we leave until morning.

Our dinner this evening is one of Leo's specialties, linguini with clams. He cooks onion, garlic, and mushrooms in olive oil. This is added to a large pot of cooked and drained noodles, along with canned clams and cubed mozzarella cheese. You stir and let it sit until the cheese melts.

The entertainment for the night includes another excerpt from Back's journal, read by Leo, and William Henry Drummond's "The Voyageur," read by Al. After everyone has meandered toward bed I walk high atop a ridge. The gray sky drizzles rain. To the south I see the last lake we were on where, nearby, a canoe still lies. To the north is the lake we will be on tomorrow. Our camp is far below next to a stand of trees. Our tiny village is miniscule, insignificant in this expanse of wild country. I am overwhelmed by the sheer space of the scene.

Most of our time is consumed with paddling, portaging, setting and breaking camp, sleeping, and eating. There is scant solitude to reflect upon where we are, the magnificence of the landscape, our distance from other humans, the wild creatures that are adapted to living here. I try to take time such as this, as often as possible, to walk away. That most of the others are content with the social aspects of the trip bewilders me. Then again, they have been friends for a long time. Or perhaps they are too tired to take strolls late at night.

*   *   *

It rains until morning. My feet and shoulders hurt so much, from hauling the canoes, I can't sleep. Aspirin does nothing. The tent is leaking—it gets worse as the journey wears on—and seems to be getting smaller. Dan and I are becoming progressively annoyed with each other in these small, uncomfortable quarters.

At breakfast Dan announces that he and I will flip a coin to see which of us carries the canoe that was left behind. The loser will carry the canoe with Leo. Why this should be narrowed down to the three of us, arbitrarily, does not cross my mind at this early hour, so I don't question the plan. Someone finds a coin and flips it. I call out, "Tails never fails." The coin comes up heads and off I trudge with Leo.

Upon returning our complainer is in rare form. "Bright morning," someone offers.

"The only things bright about this morning are my yellow teeth," he replies.

Before long we are on the water fighting a headwind and waves, from trough to crest, of at least two feet. Finally, beyond a narrow spit of land is the Hoarfrost River. This portage will be our last from a lake; those we encounter next will be around the rapids of the Hoarfrost River as we paddle upstream to Walmsley Lake.

Still far from shore, where waves are crashing on a sandy beach lined with willows, my eye catches a sturdy creature

41

bounding over the ridge toward us. It is a man, dressed completely in bright blue rain gear.

Aki, Dave and Leo

Chapter Five

Aki

*It is in deep solitude and silence that I find the gentleness
with which I can truly love my brother and my sister.*

-Thomas Merton

We know, immediately, that this is Aki, who is traveling
solo in a sea kayak. He had stopped at Olesen's cabin several
days before us and had been encouraged to try this new route.
We knew he was ahead of us, but because of his head start we
never expected to see him. Aki explains that he has been
windbound for three days here—days that we had pushed on.
He helps us carry our gear over the portage, then we brew a pot
of coffee.

Aki lives in Tokyo, among the world's largest and most
densely populated cities, and he confirms the obvious: "Big
city. Crowded."

This is his fifth trip to the Canadian north. He has taken
one other long vacation. Several years back he bicycled from

Los Angeles to Washington, D. C. in 45 days. He is on his way, now, to the mouth of the Coppermine River far to the north. He subsists mostly on fresh fish and either rice or instant mashed potatoes.

There is a certain attraction to seeing another person in such a remote area and the feeling is mutual. Aki clearly enjoys our company.

For a few minutes we are alone and I ask Aki what draws him, again and again, to this landscape. He struggles with the question. In his broken English he says that he likes open space. "No people. No hurry." The answer, however, lies in a phrase he repeats five or six times.

"Settle down," he says.

Wilderness, I believe Aki is saying, lends perspective to our everyday existence. This respite gives us a fresh, firsthand look at our world—and ourselves. We come closer to the roots of our existence. Wilderness experience lends itself to a sense of freedom, stability, inner peace, gratitude and joy.

In wilderness we appreciate that we are rather small, in the midst of a bigger picture. Indeed, we have the opportunity to settle down. To think clearly. To breathe deeply. To relax. To push ourselves physically. (These are not mutually exclusive.) To absorb our surroundings. To appreciate the forces that created the beauty before us.

But now it is time for us to move on. We leave Aki, who is in no hurry, to once again battle the wind.

Al Gustaveson

Chapter Six

A Complete Desolation,
A Northern Fairyland

*But surely we carry this civilization too far, and are in danger
of warping our natural instincts by too close observance of the
rules that some mysterious force obliges us to follow when we
herd together in big cities...A dweller in cities is too wrapped
up in the works of man to have much respect left for the works
of God, and to him the loveliness of forest and mountain, lake
and river, must ever appear but a weary desolation.*

-Warburton Pike, *The Barren Ground of Northern Canada,*
1892

Our progress is sluggish. It is so cold and damp that when
we stop for lunch we spread out a huge tarp with everyone
underneath, sitting on the edges. The upper portion of the tarp
rests on our heads, with the ends tucked in. We pass crackers,
dried fruit, and peanuts in the dry and relatively warm confines
of the tarp. I am fortunate to be on one end, although it still

feels crowded and stuffy. As soon as I finish lunch I take a walk on the island, in the rain. From a distance the makeshift cafeteria, still full of people, is a sight to behold.

The wind is stiff as the others finally emerge from the tarp. Al is not feeling well and reports some of the symptoms of hypothermia. He is shivering, feeling fatigued, and acting clumsy. We decide to call it a day and paddle just a few hundred yards to a camp spot in a swampy area.

Rain begins to fall again as Dan and I set up the tent. Dan digs deep into his pack. He finds two books for us, for which I am quite grateful, since we will have some time as we wait out the wind. One is titled, *What Am I Doing Here*? That title sums up how many in the group are feeling right now.

It is still early afternoon and we are alerted that if the wind calms down we will press on and paddle at night. With that in mind I rest, reading and sleeping, for several hours. The wind continues to howl. After dinner we are again advised that as soon as the wind abates we will move on, regardless of hour. I walk the length of the island and watch Dan haul in a 12-pound northern pike. We return to camp where everyone is asleep.

*   *   *

We are awakened at 5:00 a.m. The wind has finally died down. We break camp in a frenzy and leave without eating breakfast. The water is calm now, but the sky remains dreary. We paddle for a few hours with little conversation. Then we pull the canoes alongside each other as we rest on the water.

"Pretty country," Leo says to Al, breaking the silence.

"Pretty desolate," Al replies.

How you perceive the landscape depends considerably upon your disposition. This is especially evident in the journals of early explorers. Warburton Pike, in his travels here more than 100 years ago, described the land as bleak: "the most complete desolation that exists on the face of the earth." Yet in another mood he described the barrenlands as a "northern fairyland" and declared: "A man who has spent much time under the influence of the charm which the north exercises over everybody wants nothing better than to be allowed to finish his life in the peace and quietness which reign by the shores of the Great Slave Lake."[10] For now Al is hungry and tired, like the rest of us. His sense of wonder will return.

Eventually, the inevitable question is raised: "When are we going to eat?" Everyone is famished and we spot relatively level terrain a few minutes paddle in the direction from which we came. But Leo (and I happen to share this trait) does not like to go backwards. His preference is made clear: "I hate to lose ground."

We land at a steeper site consistent with the direction we're traveling. Someone picks up the lunch pack, takes a few steps up the near-vertical embankment, and falls down. We are too hungry to take the time to cook up hot cereal. Instead, we wolf down our standard lunch fare for breakfast.

After our meal we continue paddling upriver. We stop in a narrow length of the channel just below Cook Lake. It is too gusty to continue so we wait for a break in the wind. To pass the time, someone casts a line into the current and immediately hauls in a large lake trout. This encourages several others to grab their fishing gear, as the sun begins breaking through the clouds. With four or five people fishing, at any given time, two or three may be reeling in trout.

Having already consumed our lunch, we cook up trout and potatoes for an afternoon dinner. We are windbound and that means some time to slow down, some time for ourselves—the upside of adversity. The wind also means fewer airborne mosquitoes. With this leisure I bathe, launder clothes, hike, take photographs, and nap in the sun.

By early evening we are once again hungry so we eat our missing meal—a breakfast of granola and grapenuts. The wind finally subsides and we paddle into the evening and the rich light at the end of the day. It is breezy, but not too strong, and the temperature is ideal for paddling.

I couldn't feel much better after a long afternoon of rest. But my friend and colleague, Dan Dustin—the only other person beside Leo I knew prior to this trip—couldn't feel worse. Dustin notifies Leo that he is not feeling well, that he will ease up on paddling. After another mile or so we pull to shore for him.

Dustin walks a short distance then settles down on the tundra among clouds of mosquitoes. Although the evening is warm, he is shaking uncontrollably. I go to his duffle to get his sleeping bag, then set up his tent with Leo. We hustle him into the tent before too many mosquitoes and black flies can join him.

Dustin feels a sharp pain in his side. His symptoms include nausea, vomiting, and diarrhea. In a tiny copse of spruce we set up a tarp, near his tent, so he has a semblance of privacy in coping with his misery.

Each of us hold theories as to what may be causing Dustin such distress. Could it be food poisoning? A severe allergic reaction to all the insect bites? Is it appendicitis or some rare condition that without prompt medical attention could be life-threatening? We don't know.

Portaging in a Vast Wilderness

Chapter Seven

Rescue Free Wilderness

We fear death most when we feel that we haven't lived yet.
We're frightened that death will come like a thief in the night
before we've really had a chance to live. This fear is most real
when we are not living in the moment. If we don't find ways to
live in the now, then death is frightening because we've never
really been present to our life. We missed it and now, all of a
sudden, it's over.

The more fully we live, the easier it is to let go, to die.

-David Steindl-Rast, *Music of Silence*

Leo and Dustin were graduate students together at the University of Minnesota. Leo, after completing his doctorate, accepted a faculty position there. Dustin took a position at San Diego State University. But they stayed in touch.

In academia you publish or perish and these two collaborated to publish much of their work. They share a professional interest in wilderness management, conservation education, and environmental ethics. Inspired by the thinking of Robert Marshall, they have a particular passion for promoting recreationist self-sufficiency in wilderness. And among other things they have advocated establishing a rescue free wilderness area.[11]

A rescue free wilderness is just what it sounds like—a place where the federal land management agency would not establish and offer rescue services.

These professors believe the wilderness experience available in many of our national parks and national forests has been tainted. Many of the most popular wilderness areas, at least in the continental United States, suffer from crowding. As more and more people converge on a wilderness area, various management strategies must be adopted. For example, a limit on use is often established. This means only those people who have applied for and secured permits may venture into the area. Wilderness managers have also found it necessary to enforce many rules and regulations. These help protect the landscape, and are essential, but come at the expense of traditional outdoor recreation liberties. In some wilderness areas, certain places are off-limits and wilderness users are assigned where they camp. All of this takes away from the freedom, the challenge, and the adventure of a wilderness experience.

Leo and Dustin proposed a rescue free wilderness in a portion of Gates of the Arctic National Park and Preserve. This enormous national park is in the Brooks Range of northern Alaska, where Robert Marshall explored the landscape more than a half century ago. Marshall earned his Ph.D. in plant pathology at Johns Hopkins University. He studied the adaptations of tundra plants to the harsh landscape of the Brooks Range. He noted that only plants well-adapted to the severe conditions could survive.

The particular location has been purposely chosen. Gates of the Arctic is very remote and mostly unvisited. Only well-seasoned wilderness travelers have the outdoor knowledge and skills to venture there. The idea is to keep this area relatively uncrowded and unregulated. People who wanted to spend time there would have to be completely self-sufficient. Just as tundra plants are adapted to the extreme conditions, wilderness users would need expert knowledge and skills to face the rigors of the environment.

In *Coming Into the Country* author John McPhee recounts the perspective of a National Park Service planner involved for years with study and planning for Gates of the Arctic: "[His] total plans for the park's development—his intended use of airstrips, roadways, lodges, lean-tos, refreshment stands, trash barrels, benches—added up to zero. The most inventive thing to do, as he saw it, was nothing. Let the land stand wild, without so much as a man-made trail."[12]

Only the federal government would be restricted from search and rescue efforts which, simply, would not be established. Obviously, members of a group would do what was possible to save a comrade. The emphasis of the policy is directed at preventing the government from getting involved.

Search and rescue efforts cost the National Park Service in the range of $3 million to $4 million dollars per year. This expense is of concern to some people. The National Taxpayers Union, a Washington-based group that advocates less government spending, says that individuals who intentionally put themselves in danger should foot the bill. Their position is that "taxpayers should not subsidize thrill seekers."[13] The existence of rescue services may encourage adventurers to take on more than they are capable of.

The National Park Service has considered requiring mountain climbers, whitewater river runners, and others engaged in high risk recreation to pay for their own rescues but dropped the idea. What if someone couldn't afford the rescue?

Subsequently, some select parks, including Denali National Park and Preserve in Alaska, have instituted registration fees. This money is pooled (like insurance) and used to help finance rescues.

However, the crux of the issue transcends saving money. The idea is philosophical. The proposed rescue free wilderness is a statement. It is a stand in favor of those who want to take full responsibility for their actions. The proposal is an affirmation of the sanctity of life—what it means to *live*.

Although philosophically consistent with wilderness ideals, the rescue free wilderness proposal has not been well received. Some opponents have pointed out that such an uncontrolled area would be an invitation for people to kill themselves. I suspect if troubled individuals actually went to the bother of going all the way to Gates of the Arctic to commit suicide, they would be so inspired by the country—the mountains, the rivers, the wildlife—they would want to live after all. These suicidal individuals would return home with a passion for the goodness of life.

Other arguments against the proposal suggest the federal government would be liable for those who were badly injured or killed. Legal scholars have looked at the issue and have suggested that if potential users are made aware of the rescue free status of the area through park information services, then it would be "highly unlikely" that the National Park Service would be held liable for injuries or deaths in such a place.[14]

Leo and Dustin are quick to point out that most people are drawn immediately to what might go wrong, rather than focusing on what may go right for those who would *choose* to enter such an area. Experienced wilderness users would thrive, almost exclusively, given arrangements where they assumed their own responsibility. Historically this country has seen a litany of explorers, such as Lewis and Clark, and all those who followed on the frontier, who depended on their own wherewithal as they set into the wilderness.

Should wilderness enthusiasts today be allowed the *choice* of total self-sufficiency in this one place? In making a decision for or against this proposal there is a bottom line that is inescapable. Upon choosing such responsibility there would be no turning back; you can't change your mind.

The most vehement opponents to a rescue free wilderness insist that those foolish enough to choose such adventure would surely regret the decision if they got in trouble. The picture that is painted is one of desperation; pathetic depictions of people regretful, panicked, and afraid to die. I believe this perspective shines light on the fears of those who oppose the idea and not, actually, those who might choose such an experience.

There are those who are willing to go out into the world, to take risks, and to grow in the process. There are those who will risk losing their lives in order to gain them. At a memorial service I attended not long ago the minister said we should not be afraid to die, we should not be afraid of dying, and we should not be afraid to *live*. The more fully we embrace life, the easier it is to die, because we have lived.

But what if Dustin, who is terribly ill out here in the wilderness, really were on the doorstep of death? Would he grovel madly about his regrets? Or would his message be something else?

I know Dustin well and I believe he would die out in the wilderness with integrity. I have taken the liberty to estimate what he might do and say. First, he would say farewell to and clear away the crowd, asking that just Leo and I remain, the two who have known him the longest. Dustin would have special words for us to convey to his beloved, Kathy. I won't attempt to second guess those words. He would mention many friends. But the focus of his words would be on his boys. Dustin might say:

> Tell Andy and Adam that I love them. They know. Tell them that I am proud of them; they are wonderful sons and they mean the world to me. Tell them that if not for pushing myself I wouldn't be the father I am, I would be something much less than that. I want them to affirm life and know what it means to live.

> So ask the boys to cherish their lives, but not be afraid to *live* their lives. Tell them to take chances. To risk failure. It is the only way to grow.

> Tell them to celebrate my life and to recall those special times we have spent together. I will live on in the memory of those shared experiences.

> I will also live on in the words of my books and those who have been influenced by those words. And in the lives of my students. And my friends.

Dustin would say to reassure his boys that the show must go on. He would ask Leo and I to look out for them as best we could.

Knowing Dustin as I do it is conceivable that he would say something funny. He might quote Robert Service or John Muir or Henry David Thoreau. He would offer keen insight. He would teach not only what it means to live, but what it means to die.

No, the scene would not be pathetic, but rather one of wisdom and courage. We are all going to die and there are worse ways to go—say in a hospital hooked up to all sorts of technology among strangers—than in the beauty of the wilderness among friends.

Dustin would express gratitude for the life he lived. Then he would show anticipation for the next adventure, one bigger than all the rest.

Dustin wrote, in *The Wilderness Within*, "To me, wilderness is the logical place, indeed the ideal place, to marvel at life's unfolding, to live at life's edge. It is in wilderness that we can best discard the protective armor that shields us from life itself. It is in wilderness that we can best rejoice in the here and now."[15]

*   *   *

The next morning we get a late start out of consideration for Dustin's condition. Still in pain, after a miserable night, he rides motionless in the bow of a canoe. Cook Lake is perfectly still, providing a mirror image of the cloud formations above.

We arrive at our first portage around the rapids of the Hoarfrost River. What appears to be a short portage is actually three-quarters of a mile. Due to the calmness of the day, the mosquitoes and blackflies are horrendous. I shoulder a canoe with Leo, past sparkling, cascading waters.

As several of us return to pick up another load, Al breaks into song as we cross a mosquito-infested swamp. With shoulders hunched, knees lifting high, hips swiveling, and fingers snapping he sings about the dreaded insects: "Mosquitoes in the morning, mosquitoes in the evening, mosquitoes at supper time . . ."

The next portage around rapids is perhaps 100 yards. Aki has caught up with us and he "lines" his sea kayak; pulling it behind him, with a rope. Leo is tempted to line the canoes—to avoid having to completely unload, carry just a short distance, and re-load—but Al is against it.

Leo and I decide to line our canoe in the water anyway. With Leo pulling from the bow and with me pushing from the stern, we maneuver the canoe upstream against a swift current. My boots feel as if they are filled with cement as we clamber over slippery boulders, up to the waist in icy water. It is a wonder we aren't swept away.

The group continues paddling upstream. The next obstacle is a chute of fast water. The canoe ahead of us crosses the torrent near the top of the rapid. We follow their lead without contemplating the hazards. We paddle the canoe properly, at a slight angle and maintaining momentum, to avoid turning over in the swift water. Still, I can feel the craft almost flip as we hit the forceful current. For the canoe to swamp at this moment would be a disaster. Our gear isn't tied in and it is inconceivable that we wouldn't have lost some of our cargo downriver. Furthermore, a dunking is the last thing Dustin needs. We are lucky.

Further along, and after a tiresome portage, we make camp out of consideration for Dustin who continues to suffer. Most everyone is exhausted, sitting around next to their packs, in a stupor. Before long, Dan and I look around for a tent site. As we pitch the tent he says, "I'd sure like a drink of water."

I reply, with unreasonable hope, "I'd sure like a beer."

Within moments Olesen's plane comes into view. He circles twice, then lands on the water. He has brought his wife, Kristen, to meet us. He has also brought us 14 cans of beer.

We cook up a feast of falafel (a mid-eastern food), breaded and soy trout, rice, and pudding. The atmosphere is like a party. The blackflies and mosquitoes are dreadful, but go unacknowledged, without a complaint from anyone.

I talk with Kristen who works as a cook at a drilling site on George Lake (named after explorer George Back). Like her husband, Kristen is tall and lean.

Aki breaks out a map and shows several of us the trips he has completed throughout the Northwest Territories. He calls the north "a treasure" and assures us that he will be back next summer for his annual meditation.

Amidst all the festivity, Dustin recuperates in his tent. Leo and Olesen consider Dustin's symptoms and decide to let him stay. (As it turns out, Dustin was likely suffering from a condition known as diverticulitis, a painful, but common malady. After experiencing similar symptoms he was diagnosed with this illness after our return.)

Before long, Olesen and his wife are ready to go home. They haven't seen each other for a month, which is not uncommon during the summer. Their little time together is precious. Kristen will be back tomorrow to accompany us for the remainder of the journey. The plane takes off from the water and they fly low past our camp. I watch until the plane is out of sight, then eat the last of my fill of trout and finish my beer. Content, I settle down to sleep, listening to the cascades of the Hoarfrost River.

Group Photo

Chapter Eight

The Country, The Space, The Sky

He makes me lie down in green pastures,
He leads me beside still waters,
He restores my soul.
–Psalm 23:2-3

The following morning we paddle a short distance, then complete a half-mile portage. I have pulled a muscle in my back and find it excruciating to lift even the lightest load. Once something is on my back, however, I can transport it without too much agony. After some success hauling packs, I think I might be able to carry a canoe. One is gently eased onto my shoulders and I feel a sharp pain, like a knife in my back. I wince as the full weight rests on my shoulders. Al says that all he had to do was look at my face to realize that carrying a canoe over this and the last portage would be out of the question. What is far worse than the heavy work, I think, is not being able to do the heavy work.

We paddle a short distance upstream to face the last portage, of 18 total, on the trip. Olesen and Kristen arrive and land their plane on the calm water of Walmsley Lake.

This portage around rapids is a short one and the canoes are quickly moved and then reloaded. The sun is shining and a light breeze blows as we gather for a group photo. Then Olesen has something to say to us.

He speaks slowly and deliberately. We are gathered in a quarter moon around him, Kristen further away by the water. Olesen recounts the highlights of our voyage from Yellowknife to Walmsley Lake, more than 270 miles. The people who will come to use these canoes, he says, will appreciate our efforts, although only we know, really, the hardships of the journey.

He acknowledges the difficulty of our task, the inclement weather, the notion that no one else, save Aki, has ever traversed this route. The canoes will not be returned to Great Slave Lake, he explains, but will be stored along a lakeshore somewhere in the barrenlands. Our group is uncharacteristically silent; focused on his words, which are heartfelt.

He says, "A bunch of young yahoos probably couldn't have done what you did. It took your maturity, your experience, and your perseverance to see the expedition through." He knows we have pushed throughout the entire trip and that several of us are sick or injured.

Olesen goes on to apologize for not getting to know us better, there not being ample opportunity to become friends, although he is open to that in the future. He invites us to come back to use the canoes, to put together a trip.

He assures us, "As you look back upon this trip you will miss the country, the space, the sky." We are welcome, he repeats, to return.

His love for this land and his admiration for what we have done are evident. Choked with emotion, now, he adds, "Thanks a lot for all you have done." His breath catches in his throat. He looks down. Kristen, from a distance, is smiling gently at him. As he turns and walks away Leo thanks him for all *he* has done for us. Olesen just keeps walking. As he passes Kristen he pauses for just a moment, then walks to his plane. She follows with him. After exchanging a private farewell he paddles his plane to deeper water, to prepare for takeoff. We will not see him again.

We launch the canoes and ferry up the narrow channel in single file as Olesen motors up the lake ahead of us. Kristen has joined our canoe and is seated in front of me, beyond the gear.

After lifting off the water Olesen circles us, then flies directly overhead in the direction of his cabin. In unison we raise our paddles to the sky in tribute to a strong and gentle man—a 15 paddle salute.

We are now on Walmsley Lake and there is a wind *behind* us for the first time. We stop for lunch on an island. The breeze is sufficient to curb the mosquitoes. According to the map we have made it beyond the northern boundary where trees grow. I hurry through lunch, then walk to the end of the island where I sit alone. Aside from the breeze and water lapping the shore there is no sound, although Olesen's words still ring in my ears. Yes, I am sure I will miss all of this: the country, the space, the sky.

The country: I am in a verdant pasture of tundra greenery. I am reclining among lichens of all shades. There is a bed of tiny pink flowers next to me. This land supports wolves and caribou, grizzlies and moose. Further north, still, there are polar bears and prehistoric-looking muskoxen.

The space: In the distance I see other islands in this huge expanse of water. I can see so far that it appears the lake drops off the end of the world.   There isn't a tree in sight.   The landscape seems to reach to eternity.

The sky: Overhead, the sun is partially obscured by a cumulus cloud. I count 20 beams of light radiating, like divine fingers of light, out of the heavens. Glory be to God.

Indeed, the moment turns magic in the harmony of the country, the space, the sky. A tear wells slowly and drops from one eye, then the other.

After lunch we paddle toward our destination, Maufelly Bay. We spot two moose, a cow and her calf, swimming in front of the canoes. As they reach shore they burst out of the water, bucking and kicking up spray, then run up and over a ridge, the calf fast on the hooves of its mother.

Aki drifts farther and farther back until he is out of sight. There will be no farewell for we will not see him again. His departure is as subtle and undramatic as his appearance was sudden.

We land on a point at the mouth of Maufelly Bay about five miles short of our final destination. After dinner, several of us pick cranberries in a bog. The sky is ever-changing, shifting from aquamarine to an unusual purple hue.

Walmsley Lake

Chapter Nine

Wolf Pups

Wolves require us to look at the world through science and spirit simultaneously and to integrate thought and feeling.

If we can do that, there is hope, not just for wolves, but for humankind.

-Peter Steinhart, *The Company of Wolves*

In the morning we eat tart cranberry pancakes. We launch the canoes for the last leg of our journey under gray skies. As we paddle, Leo confides in me that he is tired, both physically and emotionally. Over the course of the expedition we have talked about our lives, our loved ones, what the future holds, various aspects of the trip—but mostly we are silent, something we are both comfortable with. However, a routine developed, not purposely, whereby several times each day one or the other of us would remark about the beauty of the land, the other person always nodding in agreement.

As we come upon a grim-looking island Leo says, "That looks like Alcatraz."

I have never heard of Alcatraz Island referred to in sublime terms. Indeed Leo, like the rest of us, is tired.

Before long we see our goal, the place we agreed to leave the canoes. The two other craft, ahead of us, land on an island, thinking it is the mainland. One of the canoeists throws his life jacket on the ground and kicks it, apparently relieved that the ordeal is over. We motion the other canoes on as we pass them and land at our last camp.

With all three canoes now on shore there are handshakes, hoots, and tears. Leo and Al embrace. After a short while, amidst considerable excitement, I am summoned to the top of a ridge. Hiking over the promontory I see a wolf den about a quarter-mile away. We keep our distance, high on the ridge, as we look down upon five young pups, a few months old. Members of our group come and go as they find out about the wolves. The pups shift around occasionally, but mostly sleep in piles of two or three. Now and then one will get up, stretch, and move to another pile.

Leo and I watch, both amazed, yet thankful for the solitude, that everyone in our party is not up on the ridge. One pup enters the den, only to re-emerge later. At the entrance of the den the pup turns its nose to the sky and howls—a long, mournful wail toward the full moon on the horizon. The pile of wolf pups increases from two, to three, to four. Then the last one joins the pack, crawling over, and settling on top of the others. Finally, one by one, they go into the den for the night. Once all of the pups are in the den we return to camp for dinner.

I eat quickly, wash a few pots and pans, fill my canteen, and return to the ridge. I am astonished, indeed overwhelmed, with what we have stumbled upon. I am hoping for a glimpse of an adult. Later in the night Leo joins me. We sit and watch a long while before retiring.

*   *   *

This last full day I take a hike with Dustin who has now recovered from his illness. We meet up with Leo a good distance from camp.

In the evening we are hit by a squall. The blast is cold, the rain is steady. Dan's tent can take no more, the middle pole snaps, and it collapses completely. We haul the tent, with a filling of sleeping bags and personal gear, under the awning of our closest neighbors and wait out the storm, telling stories in their tent. After the storm we fix Dan's tent so it will survive the last night, eat fish chowder for dinner, then fall asleep.

*   *   *

Arrangements have been made for flying back to Yellowknife and we will be picked up by a Twin Otter this evening. After breakfast I watch the wolf pups explore the terrain that lies within a few hundred yards of the den. They explore independently, then reconvene to nap in piles. Now and again they cry out.

Later in the day I make a loop hike, alone. I stop often, full of wonder. Sometimes I walk a couple hundred yards before pausing. In other instances I move forward only a few steps before stopping to look around. The scene changes constantly: The country. The space. The sky.

I am wearing a flannel shirt, sweater, vest, and parka—in July. It is a blustery day with occasional sprinkles. Once again a quiet water's edge I listen closely to the breath of the wind and nothing else.

Reflections

Chapter 10

Afterword

[W]e are told to honor the Sabbath and to keep it holy by making it a day of rest for ourselves...To honor the Sabbath means to leave a portion of time unexploited, to relinquish for a spell our moneymaking, our striving, our designs. To honor wilderness means to leave a portion of space unexploited...and to leave unharmed the creatures that dwell there. Both wilderness and Sabbath teach us humility and restraint; they put us back in touch with the source of things. They are as close as we come, in this life, to paradise.

-Scott Russell Sanders, *Arctic Refuge: A Circle of Testimony*

A wilderness experience is about time and space. Initially, we must allocate time to break away. This can be the greatest challenge—setting aside time for something we know will bring a special dimension to our lives. We have to instruct and discipline ourselves to make room for adventure that may enrich us beyond our dreams.

The adventure itself is like an extended Sabbath—a sabbatical. A sabbatical is both a time of rest and a time of ambitious creative pursuit. Similarly, adventure in our lives allows us to leave behind routine chores to actively pursue a different agenda. Part of what is so rejuvenating is the contrast to day-to-day activities and the luxury of intense focus.

A wilderness experience is also dependent upon unexploited, unmanaged and seemingly unlimited space. We find harmony of form and color and life as we fall into resonance with ancient rhythms. On this trip we were inspired by the stark beauty of a land beyond treeline.

In wilderness, we may wonder about the adaptations of various organisms to their environment and the relationships that exist among species. John Muir wrote, "Everything is so inseparably united. As soon as one begins to describe a flower or a tree or a storm ... up jumps the whole heavens and earth and God Himself in one inseparable glory!"[16]

One of the highlights of this journey was watching the wolf pups at play. I observed an innocence, unimaginable in our everyday lives, that is completely oblivious to our existence, and yet, in many ways, is dependent upon the integrity of our actions.

On this trip we were exposed firsthand to a land almost untouched by humans and we followed in the wake of early explorers to the far north. This was a history lesson without parallel. The past came to life as we practiced tasks from centuries ago. We cooked over open fires, paddled the lakes and rivers, and heard the same haunting calls of the loons. We knew the same vast horizons and the ever-changing patterns of the sky.

The very nature of a wilderness adventure suggests challenge and risk. These experiences are exhilarating and we have a greater sense of being alive. We push ourselves in wilderness to reach a goal: the top of a mountain, the depths of a canyon, a far lake. We strive hard to do something with the faith that it is worth the effort.

Yet a price is paid and that is part of the point. Across the board we faced various ailments on this trip and everyone was physically exhausted and emotionally drained by the end. Had it been a relaxing fishing excursion it wouldn't have been the same, it wouldn't have meant as much.

Hardship is part of the experience, indeed part of the attraction. An adventure without difficulty is a contradiction. A life without trial is not fully lived. The storms of our lives lend themselves to fear, anger, self-pity and despair *or* an expanded degree of gratitude for what we *do* have which translates into a sense of peace, serenity, thanksgiving and joy.

Wilderness adventure can elicit deep emotional responses. It can generate a sense of clarity and truth. Such adventure may overwhelm the senses, prompt consideration of new priorities, assist in confronting adversity, initiate a generous response, or inspire a courageous course of action. Exposure to a wild landscape may encourage a less complex, less stressful, less consumptive way of life. A wilderness odyssey can generate a sense of hope, of seeing the good in life through all of the bad.[17]

We need the contrast of adventure in our lives—some adventure—to complement our day-to-day routines and obligations. Both are essential for our well-being as are solitude and community, focused effort and relaxation, affliction and triumph. In wilderness we are capable of moving beyond what we are accustomed to seeing, feeling, thinking, and doing into new territory of the landscape and the mind.

Amidst the power and quiet of wilderness we may test and rest our minds and bodies and find our souls restored. And even though we travel through the valley of the shadow of death, we may fear no evil.[18]

*   *   *

Have you gazed on naked grandeur where there's nothing else
to gaze on,
Set pieces and drop-curtain scenes galore,
Big mountains heaved to heaven, which the blinding sunsets
blazon,
Black canyons where the rapids rip and roar?
Have you swept the visioned valley with the green stream
streaking through it,
Searched the Vastness for a something you have lost?
Have you strung your soul to silence? Then for God's sake go
and do it;
Hear the challenge, learn the lesson, pay the cost.

-Robert Service

*   *   *

Notes

[1] Olson, Sigurd, *The Lonely Land*, New York: Knopf, 1961.

[2] Nute, Grace Lee, *The Voyageur*, St. Paul: Minnesota Historical Society, 1931. Much of the historical material in this section is derived from this work and Nute's *The Voyageur's Highway*, St. Paul: Minnesota Historical Society, 1941.

[3] Back, George, *Narrative of the Arctic Land Expedition to the Mouth of the Great Fish River and Along the Shores of the Arctic Ocean in the Years 1833, 1834, and 1835*, London: John Murray, Albemarle Street, 1836.

[4] Seton, Ernest Thompson, *The Arctic Prairies*, New York: International University Press, 1911.

[5] George Back, 1836.

[6] Service, Robert, *Collected Poems of Robert Service*, New York: Dodd, Mead & Company, 1940.

[7] Robert Service, 1940.

[8] McCullough, David, "The Power of Place," *National Parks*, 76(1-2), 2002.

[9] Information in this section is derived from conversations with Dave Olesen, literature from his outfitting business, and two of his books as follows: *Cold Nights, Fast Trails*, Minocqua, WI: Northword Press, 1989 and *North of Reliance: A Personal Story of Living Beyond the Wilderness*, Minocqua, WI: Northword Press, 1994.

[10] Pike, Warburton, *The Barren Ground of Northern Canada*, New York: MacMillan and Co., 1892.

[11] Leo McAvoy and Dan Dustin have written extensively about the rescue free (no rescue) concept in resource management literature such as: "The Right to Risk in Wilderness," *Journal of Forestry*, 79(3), 1981.

[12] McPhee, John, *Coming Into the Country*, New York: Farrar, Straus & Giroux, Inc., 1976.

[13] Salant, Jonathan, "Should Thrill Seekers Pay For Rescue?" *The San Diego Union-Tribune*, A1, A13, March 11, 1999.

[14] McAvoy, Leo; Dustin, Dan; Rankin, Janna; and Frakt, Arthur, "Wilderness and Legal Liability: Guidelines for Resource Managers and Program Leaders," *Journal of Park and Recreation Administration*, 3(1), 1985.

[15] Dustin, Dan, *The Wilderness Within: Reflections on Leisure and Life*, Third Edition, Champaign, IL: Sagamore Publishing, 2006.

[16] Muir, John, quoted in Wolfe, Linnie Marsh, *Son of the Wilderness: The Life of John Muir*, Madison: The University of Wisconsin Press, 1973.

[17] A similar list of qualities is presented in a book I wrote with Ted Cable as follows: Beck, Larry and Cable, Ted, *Interpretation for the 21st Century: Fifteen Guiding Principles for Interpreting Nature and Culture*, Second Edition, Champaign, IL: Sagamore Publishing, 2002.

[18] Psalm 23

CPSIA information can be obtained
at www.ICGtesting.com
Printed in the USA
FSHW020156180920
73331FS